CAT COUTURE

JASON McGROARTY

Michael O'Mara Books Limited

To Karen McDermott, graphic designer, cat mum
and unsurpassable cat-wrangler, who keeps
Hummus's focus during our photo shoots

First published in Great Britain in 2016 by
Michael O'Mara Books Limited
9 Lion Yard
Tremadoc Road
London SW4 7NQ

A CIP catalogue record for this book is available from the British Library.

Papers used by Michael O'Mara Books Limited are natural, recyclable products made
from wood grown in sustainable forests. The manufacturing processes conform to the
environmental regulations of the country of origin.

ISBN: 978-1-910552-62-9 in hardback print format
ISBN: 978-1-910552-63-6 in ebook format

1 2 3 4 5 6 7 8 9 10

Cover and page design by Jade Wheaton

Printed and bound in Malta

www.mombooks.com

INTRODUCTION

Karen and I adopted Hummus from a cat sanctuary in Convoy, Donegal, in 2009. Although a beautiful kitten, she was the runt of the litter, always shying away from people, but she fitted into our family well and, little by little, started coming out of her shell. However, soon after she came home, she was diagnosed with feline leukaemia virus (FLV). Although FLV is very treatable, Hummus was no longer allowed to roam free, as she could easily fall ill or spread the virus to other cats.

The idea for *Cat Couture* first came about when I returned home one day, exhausted after long shoot, and thought, 'There has to be some way to keep my costs low and still develop an amazing portfolio!'... The first shot I ever took was Hippy Dippy Hummus on page 25 and I was amazed by how comfortable she was in front of the camera straight away. Hippy Dippy is one of my favourite images in the book because it marked the start of something amazing for Hummus and me.

The costumes, accessories and backgrounds are all designed, created and styled by Karen and me, using old materials and fabrics that we find around the house. Some costumes are very easy to make; others take a little longer – such as the 'Viktor & Rolf'-inspired photograph on page 45, which features a couture headpiece and gown fashioned from wire, mesh, black lace, cardboard and beads ... We feel (and Hummus agrees) it was worth the effort.

Apart from capturing 'a look', I've also tried hard to capture Hummus's wit, charm and sweetness in these shots. She uses such a range of expressions – cheeky, willful, inquisitive, demure, grumpy – and happy! – she truly is my model and muse, perfectly capturing the mood and the moment. And I'm delighted to have this opportunity to share them – and her – with you.

Jason McGroarty, Donegal

PUSS OF THE SEVEN KINGDOMS

I admit, we have had a great deal of fun coming up with the content for the book you now hold before you. However, this was *not* my favourite shoot (as you may tell from my disgruntled expression – yes, I'm looking at *you*). I have nothing against the costume – heavens, no! – I know of few other kittys that would rock this look quite so successfully. What I object to is the grated Styrofoam 'snow' He showered me with. What? How utterly pathetic! And how was I to know it was Styrofoam until I ate a few of the bigger chunks? That plastic stuff made my poor mouth quite dry and, try as I might, I couldn't get rid of the taste.

Quite a good look though, eh? Miaow!

MOGGY MONDRIAN

I am a huge fan of Piet Mondrian's work (and I'm sure the feeling would have been mutual). I know JM is fond of the De Stijl art movement, so when He mentioned that He had an idea based around the reduction to essentials of form and colour, who was I to resist? Primary colours are so – well, *me*. And a grid! Darling, you need say no more.

Of course, in this photograph JM thinks I am being quirky and cute, whereas I know that this is *exactly* what Mondrian had in mind. Other Neoplasticists came and went but Mondrian was the real deal.

And this picture is my *homage* to him.

WALL STREET

When I came on set this morning, JM had this crazy loud electro-funk blaring from the iPod. He doesn't usually discuss the scene that much beforehand, preferring instead to 'catch me unawares' with some devastating poses that might come from left field (wherever that is). Well, this morning as I composed myself and dressed, all the while searching for my motivation, I could hear Him shouting 'Show me the money!', so I knew something was afoot. It was devilishly difficult to get the tie anywhere near straight, but the dinky wings on my collar are to die for, so I'm not complaining. And here we are, the Wolf of Wall Street rides again!

GEISHA HUMMUS

'Konnichiwa' to my friends across the world! This is one of my personal favourite photographs. The colours in my kimono blend perfectly to complement my own natural colouring. I was a little concerned when JM brought the chopsticks out (it wouldn't be the first time He's caught me with a sharp jab … He says it's accidental, but …). However, it all went to plan and I think the result is stunning. See how my eyes 'pop' with colour? Ah yes, those eyes truly do follow one around the room.

QUEENLY KITTY

Now this one really did have me stumped for a while. I will not – *will not!* – wear one of those collars from the vet. I don't care what's wrong with me; I won't wear it. So when JM first approached me with this little number, I rather lashed out. Yes, I regret it now, but you can't blame me for my mistake.

Anyhoo, this, apparently, is an Elizabethan standing collar and robe. Handmade by Himself, with all the attention to detail that this kitty loves so much, once I'd got it on I didn't want to take it off! The red braiding and gold button make me feel empowered – *go* you regal feline!

FRIDA KATLO

The name Frida Kahlo was new to me, to be honest, but I know JM is a huge fan – always talking about her work and how she was such an inspiration to Him when He started out as an artist. Well, what could I say? 'Go on then,' was all that sprang to mind.

However, as you know by now, I couldn't possibly enter into the spirit of another artist without further research of my own: and frankly, I was blown away by what I found out about Ms Kahlo. Born in Mexico … indigenous art … uncompromising depiction of the female form … 'This is the gal for me!', thought I. So as you look at this portrait, I hope you can see that I plunged myself into it, even allowing Him to use a red rose (one of Frida's iconic accessories) as a hat on my head.

I think I nailed it, don't you?

COUNT CATULA

'I want to suck your *blood!*' Don't be silly, it's only me, but I'm loving this Dracula get-up – aren't you? I really do think red is my colour, and those pearls! *Bram Stoker's Dracula* is one of JM's favourite films, so this outfit was a shoe-in for the book. But as we were shooting, he kept saying 'More, give me more!' and I didn't quite know what to do. Anyway, then He had a thought and rubbed some of my favourite kitty treats at the side of my mouth so that I would lick my lips. I thought it was a cheap trick at first but wowser! Look at the result!

I'm not *really* an evil puss … I promise …

MADAME HUMMUS

This photograph was taken as a tribute to Madame Lucia Elizabeth Vestris, an opera singer, burlesque performer and theatre manager par excellence. By all accounts, Madame Vestris was a very sassy lady and a class act – two among many of the traits we have in common. And she loved a hat – as do I. Not many kitties can carry off a feathered hat but I feel I do, with aplomb!

HUMMUS POTTER

Of course I've read *Harry Potter.* Who hasn't? JM couldn't believe his luck when I donned the round glasses and went all Hogwarts on him. But, as I keep telling him, I'm a *performer* – it's just what I do.

I knew this one was coming, of course. He's read every book cover to cover several times over and he insisted that we watch the movies together time after time. Not that I mind sitting on the sofa for a few hours – that's just what I do, too.

SHIP AHOY!

A sailor's life for me! I do love this one. Sometimes I think I was built for comfort, not for speed, and this costume was divinely comfy. The T-shirt fit my contours like a glove. And the hat — it's so Gaultier, don't you think?

I want to say something about my costumes. Throughout the book you will have seen me in some awesomely stylish clothes and these are all made especially for me by my dear JM. He is such a treasure. I know I can be rude to him at times but He knows I don't mean it … Well, hardly ever. As long as He continues to make me fabulous I will be his favourite feline. There, I've said it, now move on.

HIPPY DIPPY

This was the start of it, you know. The very first shot He took of me. The moment He realized I was a star. I'm very fond of it: the colours, the bright shining eyes and that tiny blue pendant on my head, just a simple thing but so effective.

I'm gorgeous. Full stop.

SIGN OF THE TIMES

Ah, the 1970s! A floral shirt and a wistful look in a skyward direction. Once again, Hummus captures the spirit of the decade. JM, knowing that I absolutely adore a ball of twine to play with, lovingly made me a ball-of-twine necklace to wear for this shot. He's so sweet to me sometimes …

FELINE IN THE FALL

As the poet once said, 'Season of mist and mellow fruitfulness …' Autumn is a fabulous time of year. Watching the trees change colour from greens to reds, yellows and browns was where JM got the idea for this outfit. Don't get me wrong, I love the dress, it's gorgeous, and I love the necklace, sure I do … but the stand-up collar – OMG! I am one foxy feline in this outfit and I don't care who knows it!

GOING DOTTY

This mind-blowing shot is a tribute to another of JM's favourite artists, Yayoi Kusama, who has been painting and creating with polka dots since she was ten years old – and she's now 87! Do you remember her series of 'happenings', in which naked participants were painted with brightly coloured polka dots? Can you see the shock on my face when He suggested getting my kitty off? No thank you – it's kit *on* for me every time!

GOING DOTTY

This mind-blowing shot is a tribute to another of JM's favourite artists, Yayoi Kusama, who has been painting and creating with polka dots since she was ten years old – and she's now 87! Do you remember her series of 'happenings', in which naked participants were painted with brightly coloured polka dots? Can you see the shock on my face when He suggested getting my kitty off? No thank you – it's kit *on* for me every time!

ICE QUEEN

Bow to me, puny human: I am the Ice Queen! I am so tempted to go outside right now and let the other cats in the neighbourhood get a load of this! There'd be no question of who was top of the pecking order.

I know I shouldn't say it, but you can see the class in me now, can't you? I simply ooze sophistication and, frankly, I was born to wear clothes like this. Move over, ma'am, there's a new queen in town!

A note of caution to any aspiring models, though: you have to be supremely gifted to carry off this look, have the patience of a saint and a certain noble breeding. So scat!

AUDREY CATBURN

I love this shot. I know I shouldn't say it, but I *love* this shot! We'd had a long day in the studio, He had had me in and out of innumerable costumes and by this time I wasn't talking to Him – I'd really had enough. But … somehow He manages to catch me in just the right pose – sparkling, wistful eyes; ears pert and alert to the slightest sound; whiskers all present and correct. That collar looks as if it were made for me (which, in fact, it was) and the golden studs – a masterstroke!

JEDI

Can you feel the force? Move over, Obi-Wan, there's a new Jedi in town! I really feel I caught the mood here. Of course, JM loves the whole *Star Wars* thing to bits so I wanted to make this one work, just for him. See? I'm an old softie really.

Give me a light saber and I'll give any menace a run for his money.

MISTRESS OF THE MANOR

At last, a portrait that nods towards my aristocratic ancestry. Apparently Rembrandt's portraiture was JM's inspiration for this one – earthy tones, brooding emotion and a lovely silver necklace – I know exactly what he means!

1980s PROM NIGHT

Erm … this one's not one of my favourites, let's leave it at that …

HIPSTER DUDE

Did you know Hipsters were a thing? I didn't, but I'm told I carry it off rather well in this shot. I love the floral shirt, I even like the necklace but why JM had to keep whispering 'psst … psst …' off-camera to make me look at Him all the time, I'll never know. He loves this finished shot but I think I look a little dazed and confused … Maybe that was the idea …

HEADPIECE HEAVEN

This one was inspired by a Viktor & Rolf ready-to-wear collection … Well, I was ready, and I wore it! You wouldn't believe how much lace and velvet was used to make this costume. I fought against wearing the headpiece for a while but in the end I'm glad I did as it captures the real me: the innocent look of that cameo brooch set against the steely, determined eyes of sweet pusskins Hummus.

It helped that He had a handful of kitty treats to offer me during the shoot, I won't deny it. A girl has to have some pleasures in life!

KITTY HENDRIX

Very occasionally I wish I had opposable thumbs, as I would have loved to play the guitar like Jimi. So when JM suggested this one, I was well up for it. The shirt I'm wearing was on the tight side, to be honest, possibly because I'd just managed to gorge myself on the treat sack in the kitchen cupboard (I don't often get the chance, so when the opportunity arose – why not?), but that bandana – OMG! – Rock Goddess or what?!

SHY HUMMY

So, throughout this book I've brought you bold, bright, dominant, strident, fearsome – all manner of looks to show off my foxy feline ways. With this one, we wanted to go into mellow mode and show the shy and retiring side of my mega personality. I can be a real pussycat, you know. Just ask JM how He feels when I gently stroke his cheek to wake him up in the mornings. Ask him how He feels when I sit on his lap and purr.

I know I might moan about him at times, but He is a sweetie and I love him to bits. Not many cats would put up with the things I have to, granted, but JM has made me a star.

SPACE COUTURE

Take me to your leader! I'm utterly mesmerizing, aren't
I? Another favourite of mine, this photograph captures
my best side. Yes, that's it, straight on, full frontal, perfect
symmetry with a hint of the ethereal: ground control
to major tomcat. This one's got the lot: shooting stars,
a black hole backdrop – and that collar! Excuse me for
saying it, but it's a killer look from a killer kat!

EATON COUTURE

Well, this one is ca-raa-zy! I nearly choked when JM came towards me with the collar – 'Me? Wear that?' To me it's a bit New Romantic – remember them? Great tunes, great times. But He tells me it's inspired by the work of 'Roadkill Couture' artist Jess Eaton (I thought it a bit distasteful myself – I mean, s*** happens to a cat, right?), but He reassured me and told me all about her. She 'repurposes' the skin, bones, whatever, of dead animals found by the road into clothing, hats and accessories. They really are amazing as well! So, this one's for you, Jess!

DIVINE DIVA

With that look on my face you'd think twice about crossing me, wouldn't you? Don't worry, that was the look I was aiming for. Sometimes I have to 'kick against the pricks', as the old saying goes, just to reassert my authority. So, when JM annoyed me with some trivial matter on the morning of this shoot, I decided to give him what for with a bit of badass bravura.

Again, nailed it. 😉

TRIBAL TIGRESS

The inspiration for this picture comes from the Baiga tribe from India. The Baiga use deep red colours, chains and feathers in their clothing, so we both felt we had to do something for the portfolio with this theme. At first He dressed me up in all sorts of robes — I was quite literally awash with reds — but when I insisted on more research He saw my point: the Baiga keep their clothing items to a bare (aha!) minimum, so off came the robes and it's a Hummus more au naturel that you see before you.

Now, where's the nice birdy?

PETAL PERFECTION

This piece is from my spring/summer collection. The palette is subtle and spare, the flowers are in full bloom, and I'm licking my lips at the thought of chomping down on a lovely lily or nibbling on a nasturtium. Some people like to look at flowers; others arrange them artfully. I simply love to eat them. I don't know what it is about the taste, but I love it. JM gets a bit frustrated when I sit next to the vase and help myself, but let's face it, there are worse hobbies!

CLEOCATRA

Cleopatra and I have quite a lot in common, you know: power, beauty and passion to name but three of the more commonplace qualities. She was famously intelligent, known for her quick wit and conversation, and wonderfully fashionable – all things that can be attributed to *moi aussi*. In this shot He dressed me in simple tones with two statement pieces that say it all really.

PS And then there's our names. She was Cleopatra, Queen of Egypt; I am Hummus, Queen of Egyptian foods. We're practically twins.

PUNK GLAM

Of course, I'm far too young to remember the birth of punk, back in the 1970s, but I love the raw energy and that whole angry, rebellious sub-culture thing. A few spiky jewels, a hardcore look and a groovy bit of tartan … what's not to love?

Some moments from our working day …